Enchanted Giving

A Winter Holiday Gift Guide

Genevive Moss

Contents

Introduction

The holiday season sparks a spirited ritual of generosity and care as people across cultures bestow thoughtful gifts upon loved ones. However, finding the perfect present can also come with stress when our good intentions to express affection falter. Cultural blunders, last-minute scrambles, and spending over budget can strain relationships rather than uplift them. As we become consumed with creating picture-perfect moments, we lose sight of what truly nourishes bonds - meaningful gestures straight from the heart.

In this guide, we'll explore the art of mindful gift-giving to spread joy without the fatigue, worry, and waste that often comes with holiday consumerism. You'll discover practical tips for discerning meaningful gifts tailored to recipients' values that feel personal rather than grabbed off a shelf. We'll navigate cultural nuances to avoid faux pas, decode subtle clues in conversations, and tap into inspiration from ancient solstice symbols and modern traditions alike. With an eye toward sustainability, you'll learn to give modest surprises that spark lasting memories out of everyday items, and support causes recipients care about in their honor.

My hope is that, with these insights, your holiday season will overflow with the true spirit behind gift exchanges - cherishing people we hold dear. Our thoughtful presents can build bridges, spark inspiration, heal rifts, and express profound gratitude for those who light our lives. May this guide help you curate gifts from the heart to nurture your most valuable relationships not just in winter, but all year long.

How to Use This Guide

F inding the perfect gift requires truly knowing someone's unique interests, values, and traditions. While this guide offers suggestions, your insight into recipients ignites the magic. See our ideas as conversation starters you can build upon.

To remain accessible, we focused on generic presents readily available to average American shoppers during the late-fall and early winter season. While technology and trends constantly shift the consumer landscape, these classic concepts express thoughtfulness across cultures and ages.

You'll find:

- Gift ideas respecting diverse holiday traditions from Christmas to Lohri to the Yule

- Suggestions honoring recipients of all backgrounds and faiths

- Ideas valuing purpose-driven professions like teaching, healthcare and sustainability

- Recommendations for major personality types in your life like creatives, intellectuals and adventurers

- Gifts tailored toward interests from books, to gardens, to stargazing

- Blank lists to help you organize your ideas and gifts.

While lovingly chosen gifts show you understand someone's essence, respect their differences if unsure. Give in ways uplifting their values. Most importantly, know your thoughtfulness outshines any particular item.

Use these spark points as a compass guiding you toward nurturing relationships. Shape suggestions to lives intricately entwined with yours. Ultimately, you supply the magic making this season glow.

A Gentle Warning

The act of gift-giving carries great power and responsibility. While presented with care and love, an inappropriate or assumption-laden present can offend rather than inspire. Many factors make up our intricate identities - faith, ethnicity, past experiences and values both spoken and unspoken. Tread carefully by considering recipients in their full and wondrous complexity.

Do not presume affiliations, interests or needs based on outward traits. Avoid gifting items conflicting with beliefs or life circumstances unless expressly desired. Seek clarity over guessing to ensure your thoughtfulness uplifts.

This guide attempts to honor the diverse holidays and personalities enriching our communities. But no one list captures any individual's beautiful multitudes. Let these act as inspiration you build upon through knowing beloveds profoundly before bestowing symbolic gifts.

If uncertainty gives you pause this season, consider more neutral offerings like consumables, donations to causes or gift cards/cash for maximum choice. Most powerfully, a card expressing your gratitude and support suffices when in doubt. For at its essence, a gift originates from cherishing connections over purchasing possessions.

Please use this cautionary preface as encouragement for celebrating people in their intricate fullness. Do so with respect, discretion and revelations offered through relationship so your thoughtfulness nourishes bonds stretching long beyond winter.

Gift Ideas for Holidays

Gifts that celebrate the holidays and beyond.

Universal Winter Giving

The winter season brings beautiful and diverse religious and cultural celebrations that many enjoy commemorating with loved ones. To help you thoughtfully honor friends and family, we've gathered gift ideas for those who may celebrate Christmas, Hanukkah, Omisoka, Kwanzaa, Dongzhi, Candlenights, Yule, Makar Sankranti, Soyal, Bodhi Day, or Lohri.

Please note this is not an exhaustive list of winter holidays, and one should never assume another's religious affiliation. This guide is simply meant to provide respectful gift inspiration if you know a recipient observes a particular tradition. The spirit of gift-giving lies in cherishing connections, upholding traditions, and spreading light during the darkest months.

You may notice some overlap with items appropriate for different celebrations. Holiday rituals often share symbolic themes across cultures like the victory of light over darkness, the gathering of loved ones, and expressing gratitude at year's end. Hopefully the varied gift suggestions below capture those universal messages in ways unique to each observance.

Bodhi Day Gifts

Bodhi Day is a Buddhist holiday celebrating the enlightenment of the Buddha. It commemorates Prince Siddhartha Gautama's meditative awakening under the bodhi tree in 596 BCE, through which he attained nirvana and grasped the roots of human suffering.

Representing the Buddha's journey to spiritual liberation, Bodhi Day inspires the Buddhist precepts of mindful living. Traditions include meditating, studying the Buddhist dharma, chanting sutras to uproot ignorance, decorating ficus trees with lights to represent the tree of awakening, and exchanging handmade gifts.

Thoughtful Bodhi Day presents reflect Buddhist principles. Popular gift ideas include prayer beads for spiritual centering, singing bowls producing healing tones, the eight auspicious symbols arranged flowers signifying harmony between humans and nature, incense purifying spaces, books encouraging peace within reach, and donations furthering compassion.

Dates celebrated:

- Same dates annually

- December 8

Gift Ideas:

- Mindfulness journal

- Bamboo tea box filled with flowering botanical blends

- Natural sandalwood mala beads

- Singing bowl tuned to the OM frequency

- Bonsai sculpted ficus miniature tree

- Framed sanskrit mantra

- Print of the Buddha with kalasha and dharmachakra mudras

- Subscription to a Buddhist periodical

- Vegetarian cookbook or freshly baked semolina and walnut kourambiethes cookies

- Donation to a relief fighting hunger through mindfulness

Candlenights Gifts

Candlenights is a secular winter holiday celebrating joy, togetherness and the light within every person. Originating from a podcast called "My Brother, My Brother, and Me," it has grown as a holiday for anyone seeking inclusive and uplifting traditions during the December season.

The concept envisions people gathering on the darkest night of the year to exchange thoughtful gifts, feast on delicious foods, and spend quality time with loved ones. Central themes shine through - embracing our inner light, displaying kindness toward all people regardless of differences, and spreading hope.

Unique traditions allow participant creativity. Many adorn homes with vibrant decorations, candles and lamps in lieu of a tree. Bell caroling, songs both nostalgic and modern, hot cocoa, fancy flannel attire and mystically inspired crafts also feature prominently. It is common for participants to make up wild and silly rumors for their own traditions, claiming that it has been practiced for centuries.

Gifts at Candlenights often promote warmth, coziness and self-care, display dazzling colors, or donate toward causes that spread light. The spirit lies in uplifting gestures that kindle connection.

Dates celebrated:

- Candlenights starts and ends for each person at different times, is about different things for each person, and is celebrated differently by each person.

Gift Ideas:

- Glass prism light catchers

- Winter white faux fur throw

- Peppermint bark bites

- Ceramic mugs painted with encouraging words

- Cozy pair of patterned socks

- Cinnamon vanilla scented candle

- Compass etched with inspiring quote

- Coloring book benefiting children's charity

- Handwritten cards expressing hope

Christmas Gifts

Christmas is an annual Christian holiday commemorating the birth of Jesus Christ. It is celebrated every December 25th by nearly 160 countries worldwide. The name derives from Old English "Cristes maesse" meaning "Christ's mass." Decorating Christmas trees, exchanging presents, caroling, attending church services, and getting together with family are hallmarks of the holiday.

In America, Christmas celebrations embrace religious origins while also representing secular values like the winter solstice, family bonding, and spiritual renewal. Popular presents reflect themes of hope, thoughtfulness, tradition, winter coziness and expressing kindness to those in need.

Dates celebrated:

- Same dates annually

- December 25

Gift Ideas:

- Ornamental nativity scene for the mantel

- Subscription to a Christmas movie streaming service

- Hot cocoa bomb treats

- Slipper socks

- Donation to charities fighting hunger and homelessness

- Handknit scarf and hat set in festive colors

- Evergreen-scented jar candles with pinecone decor

- Ticket to a local performance of the Nutcracker ballet

- Cookbook of classic Christmas dessert recipes and holiday traditions

- Star tree topper symbolizing hope and generosity

Dongzhi Gifts

Dongzhi, one of the most important Chinese holidays, celebrates the arrival of winter and the longest night of the year. Marking the end of fall harvests, it carries themes of unity, gratitude, family reunion and renewal.

Literally translating to "extreme of winter," Dongzhi has over 2,000 years of history in China. The origins lie in yin and yang philosophy - in order to welcome spring and longer days, people endure and find meaning during the winter solstice and darkness. Now the holiday is enjoyed among Asian communities globally.

Traditions include ornate decorations evoking the sun and longer days ahead, eating hot pot or tangyuan rice balls, burning incense to venerate ancestors, and gathering with loved ones to exchange well wishes and symbolic gifts like oranges and heated rocks representing warmth.

Popular presents also include sunlight-inspired jewelry and crafts, treats to share like persimmons for good fortune and tea for wisdom, shimmering candles welcoming new beginnings and donations to environmental efforts working to preserve the sacred balance of the seasons.

Dates celebrated:

- Falls on the shortest day and longest night of the year

- 2023: December 22, 2023

- 2024: December 21, 2024

- 2025: December 21, 2025

Gift Ideas:

- Vibrant Dongzhi lanterns

- Box of ripening persimmons

- Sweet and savory mooncake flavors

- Handwarmers or heated eye masks

- Photo book celebrating past generations

- Green tea blend promoting mindfulness

- Citrus-scented essential oil candle

- Origami decorations representing vitality

- Fair trade silk shawl in crimson or gold

- Donation supporting climate change education

Hanukkah Gifts

Hanukkah, also known as the Festival of Lights, is a 8-day Jewish holiday commemorating the rededication of the Second Temple in Jerusalem in the 2nd century BCE. When Judah Maccabeus and his followers liberated the temple, they found only enough untainted sacred oil to keep the menorah's candles burning for a single day. Yet the flames miraculously lasted for eight nights, giving them enough time to find more oil.

Hanukkah celebrates the themes of light overcoming darkness, the miracle of perseverance against all odds, and the ultimate triumph of good over evil. Traditions include lighting the nine-branched Hanukkiah each evening, eating foods fried in oil like latkes and sufganiyot, and playing the dreidel game.

In America, Hanukkah has also become a time to exchange gifts across eight nights, often focusing on educational presents or gelt, which represents gold coins. Families also honor the historic struggle for liberty through songs, stories, and solidarity.

Dates celebrated:

- Beginning on the Hebrew calendar date of 25 Kislev, and lasting for eight days

- 2023: Starts at sundown on December 7, 2023 and ends with sundown on December 15, 2023

- 2024: Starts at sundown on December 25, 2024 and ends with sundown on January 2, 2025

- 2025: Starts at sundown on December 14, 2025 and ends with sundown on December 22, 2025

Gift Ideas:

- Hanukkiah candle holders or oil lamps

- Dreidels and gelt (chocolate coins)

- Books on Hanukkah traditions

- Tickets to a virtual cooking class to learn making latkes or sufganiyot

- Family board games

- Hanukkah decorations like festive tablecloths, napkins or menorah plates

- Donation to a Jewish charity or cultural organization on their behalf

- Subscription box featuring items made by Jewish creators

- Custom-made holiday candles or soap

- Accessories featuring blue and white decorative motifs

Kwanzaa Gifts

K wanzaa is an annual 7-day celebration of African American culture and values that takes place from December 26th to January 1st. Dr. Maulana Karenga, professor and chair of Black Studies at California State University, founded Kwanzaa in 1966 during the Black Freedom Movement to honor and uplift African heritage.

Kwanzaa brings families and communities together through the Nguzo Saba, or seven guiding principles. Each night, participants light one of the seven candles in the kinara which represent unity, self-determination, collective work and responsibility, cooperative economics, purpose, creativity and faith. Other traditions include decorating homes with African art and textiles, exchanging handmade gifts, feasting on traditional dishes, playing African drums, telling stories about ancestors and celebrating black accomplishments.

Popular presents that embrace Kwanzaa's values include homemade goods showcasing craftsmanship and creativity, goods from black-owned businesses, African inspired clothing and accessories made through fair trade, children's books highlighting black leaders and heroes, tickets to cultural events that unite the community and donations to non-profits advancing social justice.

Dates celebrated:

- Same dates annually

- December 26 – January 1

Gift Ideas:

- Kinara candle holders with seven candles

- Handwoven Kente cloth blankets or scarves

- Cookbooks featuring African diaspora recipes

- Black artisan blending teas

- Subscription box from minority-owned business

- Wood carved symbols of "lifecycle" figurines

- Family journal or scrapbook celebrating ancestors

- Jar of homemade vanilla chai tea mix

- Tickets to a museum exhibition on African culture

- Donation to youth education or economic equality programs

Lohri Gifts

Lohri is a popular winter Punjabi folk festival celebrated in India and by the Sikh community worldwide. Occurring in January, it honors the ending of the winter season and the upcoming harvest. It is part of the same festival celebrated for Makar Sankranti, but honored in different areas of the world with different intent.

Traditions include lighting bonfires, feeding them peanuts, sesame seeds and sugar cane meant for a sweet year ahead, wearing flower garlands, singing and dancing bhangra around the fire, feasting on festive sarson da saag with makki di roti cornbread and exchanging sesame sweets and puffed rice mixtures as token snacks perhaps signifying dormant seeds stirring back to life. Other practices are similar to the American traditions of caroling and trick-or-treating.

In India, Lohri gifts might include shawls, jewelry, household items, or sewing machines wishing prosperity. Other thoughtful presents could be winter fruits like sugarcane or wool items keeping the cold weather at bay. In America, Lohri celebrations focus on community, lifting each other up and carrying on resilient ancient rituals even across oceans.

Dates celebrated:

- It is observed in the month of Poh and is set by the solar part of the lunisolar Punjabi calendar and in most years it falls around 13 January of the Gregorian calendar.

- 2023: (complete at the time of publication) January 14, 2023

- 2024: January 13, 2024

- 2025: January 13, 2025

Gift Ideas:

- Strings of dried orange chilies and marigolds

- Woolen scarves, hats and socks

- Bronze diyas decorated with peacocks

- Packs of peanuts, sesame seeds and puffed rice

- Collections of folk songs performed during Lohri

- Sewing boxes with vibrant embroidery thread

- Fair trade woven cotton shawls

- Incense sticks with spicy aromas

- Books with illustrations of Lohri traditions

- Donations to a campaign upholding religious diversity

Makar Sankranti Gifts

Makar Sankranti is a Hindu solar kite festival celebrating the start of Uttarayan, the sun's journey north, and the end of the winter solstice. Marking longer, warmer days ahead, it represents renewal, prosperity and auspicious beginnings. It is part of the same festival celebrated for Lohri, but honored in different areas of the world with different intent.

Traditions trace back to the Rig Veda and honor the Hindu sun gods Surya and Agni. Across India and Nepali communities worldwide, people fly festive kites, feast on sweet sesame treats, honor ancestors and holy rivers like Ganga, exchange texts praying for peace and prosperity, light diyas in vibrant colors, and give thanks for future prosperity.

Gifts signify renewal, bright horizons and hopes fulfilled. Popular presents include sesame or rice treats to share sweet beginnings, intricately decorated kites symbolizing reaching ambitious heights, cozy blankets or clothing keeping winter's chill at bay, inspirational journals and quills for manifesting intentions, eco-conscious prayer candles and donations to humanitarian efforts building a brighter tomorrow.

Dates celebrated:

- Same dates annually

- January 14 – January 15

Gift Ideas:

- Sweet and savory homemade til ke laddu

- Fair trade patchwork throw blanket

- Pack of nag champa incense sticks

- Etched copper diya lamps

- Kite reels and vibrant silk prayer kites

- Hand carved rosewood journal with note cards

- Brass pen stand and feather quills

- Unity bracelets made with seven threads

- Book or DVD of indian children's stories

- Donation to the a foundation working to nourish under-served school children

Omisoka Gifts

O misoka is the Japanese Buddhist custom of reflecting on the passing year and cleansing for the future during New Year's Eve. Meaning "big last day," celebrations focus on releasing the unfinished baggage of the past.

Rituals include visiting temples to hear 108 resounding gong chimes purifying worldly desires, gathering round a kadomatsu pine tree gate representing virtue and longevity, feasting on buckwheat noodles symbolizing prosperity, contemplating nature's cycles through seasonal poetry and chanting "joya no kane" on temple bells encircling midnight to welcome an auspicious rebirth.

Thoughtful gifts respectfully embrace the hopeful themes. Ideas include pine-scented candles honoring resilience enduring winter's frost, handmade udon noodle kits signifying fortune, poetry anthologies and calligraphy brushes for crafting cathartic art, decorative wind chimes, flutes and drums spreadings meditation through music, mindfulness journals for intention setting and donations promoting spiritual healing across communities.

Dates celebrated:

- Same dates every year

- December 31

Gift Ideas:

- Mindful gardening kits to plant daffodil bulbs

- Buckwheat soba noodle rolling pins and imported flour

- Haiku poetry collections

- Handmade soaps and shamisen washing boards

- Peace cranes folded from recycled origami paper

- Incense holders shaped like cherry blossoms

- Digital nature sound machines with bell chants

- Bamboo fountain pens and mindfulness planners

- Lucky daruma figurines made of papier-mâché

- Donations helping provide Omisoka bell ringing ceremonies globally

Soyal Gifts

S oyal is the most important winter celebration in the Zuni and Hopi traditions. Marking the start of the winter solstice and beginning of longer days, it carries themes of renewal, purification, initiation rights and sacred dance.

Central to Soyal is the lighting of fires in kivas to welcome back the sun. Other rituals include fasting, prayer sticks, venerating ancestors and the spirit world, kneeling on the ground to show humility, dances asking nature's forgiveness for harming the earth, and ceremonies initiating youth into adulthood.

Gifts embody the symbols of Soyal. Thoughtful gift ideas include blankets signifying warmth and shelter, handwoven baskets reflecting patience and prayers offered to Mother Earth, jewelry crafted from materials mined respectfully, flutes played in ceremonies, books on indigenous science sustaining communities for centuries and donations to native-led conservation efforts preserving sacred land and culture.

Dates celebrated:

- Falls on the shortest day and longest night of the year

- 2023: December 22, 2023

- 2024: December 21, 2024

- 2025: December 21, 2025

Gift Ideas:

- Rabbit fur and turquoise mosaic pouches

- Blue corn and agave salt scrub

- Stone etched with Zuni sun symbol

- Natural wooden clock carved with petroglyph designs

- Hopi pottery with traditional iconography

- Pack of heirloom Hopi blue cornmeal

- Turquoise beaded bracelet or mosaic pendant

- Family games celebrating indigenous heritage

- Roasting sticks for making chimaki bread

- Donation to a tribal coalition protecting sacred sites like the Grand Canyon

Yule Gifts

Yule celebrates the winter solstice and the rebirth of the sun in pagan and Wiccan winter traditions. Also known as Alban Arthan, Saturnalia, Midwinter, or the Return of Light, it honors themes of renewal, unity, reflection, and spiritual awakening.

Marking the longest night and shortest day, Yule carries symbolic meaning - even through bitter cold and darkness, brighter fortunes ahead can be trusted, similar to the coming warmth of spring. Common rituals include burning the Yule log, hanging mistletoe and holly, singing ancient carols of the Oak and Holly Kings battling for the glowing sun wheel, and gathering to feast on seasonal delicacies.

Gifts embody the shifting seasons. Popular presents include evergreen wreaths and decor symbolizing enduring life, sweet treats and wine for toasting long winter nights, cozy items bringing literal and spiritual warmth, token gifts handmade from nature and donations supporting conservation protecting sacred green spaces.

Dates celebrated:

- Falls on the shortest day and longest night of the year

- 2023: December 22, 2023

- 2024: December 21, 2024

- 2025: December 21, 2025

Gift Ideas:

- Gold leaf chalices for ceremonial wine

- Pine cone fire starters

- Handknit scarf in crimson or emerald

- Custom blend of warming chai spices

- Cedarwood essential oil soap

- Yearlong calendar for bullet journaling

- Glass blown ornament tree with nature motifs

- Winter bird seed mix and feeders

- Book on ancient solstice traditions

- Donation to forest restoration nonprofit

Gift Ideas for Professions

Gifts that celebrate the ones who make a difference.

Gratitude for Service

This gift guide provides suggestions for those in service roles who you may frequently interact with but don't know personally. While professional codes often prevent accepting presents, a small token of thanks can often uplift anyone's day. Of course, not all people wish to combine their personal and professional lives. These are merely ideas should you wish to gift those enhancing your everyday experiences.

So please, kindly respect all gift policies and desires.

You'll find inspirations for education, healthcare, hospitality, delivery workers, personal services, customer service, maintenance staff, and more. Some concepts can repeat across groups, as certain gifts express appreciation universally. But your gratitude outshines any particular item.

Please use this guide to thoughtfully honor these everyday heroes who so often go unseen.

Gifts for Beauty Pros

Stylish gear:
- Makeup brush sets
- Haircut capes
- Tool storage cases

Industry guidance:
- Virtual tutorials
- Online software access
- Expert coaching sessions

Thoughtful DIY presents:
- Customized makeup palettes
- Monogrammed aprons
- Handmade appointment books

Support important causes:

- Esthetician school funds

- Grooming services for people in need

- Promoting public skin health education

Gifts for Delivery Workers

Functional gear:

- Insulated bags & coolers

- Ergonomic accessories

- Custom tote organizers

Job aids:

- Navigation & mapping apps

- Delivery management software

- Professional development funds

Thoughtful DIY presents:

- Personalized hydration bottles

- Handmade appreciation kits

- Gift baskets with snacks

Support important causes:

- Relief funds for injured workers

- Fair compensation advocacy

- Mental health resources

Gifts for Education & Healthcare Staff

Essential supplies:

- Premium teacher resource bundles

- Gift certificate for a teacher supply store

- Stationery set

Self-care treats:

- Wellness or meditation apps

- Personal trainers or fitness instructors

- Audiobook memberships

Thoughtful DIY presents:

- Handmade personalized cards

- Custom mentorship journals

- Student appreciation cards

Support their efforts:

- Classroom enrichment funds

- Nursing continuing education

- Caregiver mental health initiatives

Gifts for Home Service Providers

Helpful tools:

Organizing bins & storage

- Ergonomic cleaning gadgets

- Protective workwear

Professional development:

- Industry software access

- Online courses

- Coaching sessions

Thoughtful DIY presents:

- Customized cleaning caddies

- Handmade spa products

- Personalized thank you notes

Support important causes:

- Fair labor advocacy

- Environmental sustainability in the home

- Entrepreneurial grant programs

Gifts for Hospitality Staff

Pampering presents:

- Spa and massage vouchers

- Luxury bath products

- Plush slippers

Helpful tools:

- Customized cleaning caddies

- Monogrammed luggage tags

- Beverage cooling tumblers

Unique experiences:

- Mixology classes

- Language workshops

- Global cuisine tours

Thoughtful DIY touches:
- Handmade candles

- Personalized coasters

- Embroidered aprons

Support important causes:
- Scholarship funds

- Safety training programs

- Financial relief for struggling staff

Gifts for Office & Security Staff

P roductive tools:

- Ergonomic desk accessories

- Laptop stands

- Organization stationery

Professional development:

- Public speaking workshops

- Industry conferences

- Leadership training

Thoughtful DIY gestures:

- Personalized planners

- Handmade self-care baskets

- Baked goods & snack kits

Support meaningful causes:

- Mental health resources

- Career development initiatives

- Workplace diversity & inclusion

Gifts for Personal Caregivers

Handy gear:

Premium diaper bags

- Ergonomic stethoscopes

- Soothing weighted blankets

Self-care essentials:

- Spa and massage vouchers

- Healthy meal delivery services

- Mental health resources

Uplifting DIY gestures:

- Handmade bath bombs

- Personalized gratitude journals

- Children's custom artworks

Support their important efforts:

- Early childhood education funds

- Caregiver mental health initiatives

- Health aide scholarship programs

Gifts for Pet Care Pros

Practical tools:

- Premium pet grooming supplies

- Comfortable shoes

- Customizable gear bags

Helpful services:

- Continuing education funds

- Veterinary software access

- Online certification courses

Thoughtful homemade presents:

- Personalized aprons

- Engraved stethoscope tags

- Baked pet treat jars

Support important efforts:

- Animal rescue & rehabilitation

- Low cost veterinary care programs

- Pet therapy initiatives

Gifts for Social Services Staff

Self-care essentials:

- Massage and spa vouchers
- Healthy meal delivery credits
- Mindfulness journal kits

Professional development:

- Industry conferences
- Language learning workshops
- Leadership training courses

Thoughtful homemade gestures:

- Appreciation baskets
- Stress relief care packages

- Customized desktop plants

Support their values:

- Donations to favorite charities

- Funds assisting vulnerable groups

- Initiatives empowering communities

Gift Ideas for Personality Types

Whether they're whimsical, wise, or just plain wonderful.

Appreciating Personality

G ifting for varying personalities allows honoring unique spirits when personal details are unknown. We explored present ideas for 10 common traits to spark inspiration:

The Adventurer, The Athlete, The Creative, The DIYer, The Homebody, The Organizer, The Philanthropist, The Pragmatist, The Sentimentalist, and The Social Butterfly.

Of course most people embody multiple qualities, but these create a foundation to relate. Some suggestions overlap, as versatile items hold diverse meanings.

With so many wondrous facets shaping our identities, consider these springboards rather than definitions. Snowflakes differ, but certain thoughtful gestures may resonate across temperaments.

Use guiding intuitions to gift in ways uplifting values verbalized or silently held. Most importantly, know your sincerity outshines any particular present.

We hope these touchpoints allow giving even without familiarity to spread generosity through your community and beyond this season.

Gifts for The Adventurer

Essential gear:

- Personalized passport cases

- Multi-tool gadgets

- Scratch-off map posters

Unique experiences:

- Surprise destination tickets

- Outdoor excursions

- Culinary adventures

Services & subscriptions:

- Luggage shipping memberships

- Travel booking credits

- Language learning platforms

Thoughtful DIY gifts:

- Custom souvenir memory jars

- Handmade travel journals

- Personalized first aid kits

Support meaningful causes:

- Clean water initiatives

- Youth outdoor education

- Sustainable tourism projects

Gifts for The Athlete

Essential gear:

- Athletic shoes & apparel

- Fitness trackers

- Gym bags and water bottles

Unique fitness experiences:

- Sports massage sessions

- Healthy Cooking classes

- Personal training

Motivational items:

- Workout programs

- Nutrition e-books

- Fitness magazines

Thoughtful DIY gifts:

- Custom foam rollers

- Handmade resistance bands

- Workout journals

Support meaningful initiatives:

- Youth sports scholarships

- Building accessible playgrounds

- Adaptive sports programs

Gifts for The Creative

Essential art supplies:

- Quality sketchbooks

- Paints, brushes, canvases

- Crafting toolkits

Career development opportunities:

- Commission pieces for the giftee

- Studio space rentals

- Feature articles or purchase ad space advertising the giftee's services

Artistic inspiration:

- Magazine subscriptions

- Online tutorial access

- Creative collaboration platforms

Thoughtful DIY presents:
- Handmade art supply organizers

- Personalized smocks

- Custom artwork jewelry

Support meaningful art causes:
- Community center funding

- Youth art education initiatives

- Diversity and inclusion art programs

Gifts for The DIYer

Essential tools:

- Quality power drills

- Toolboxes and belts

- Good Knee pads

Home improvement guidance:

- Consultations with contractors

- Virtual interior design services

- Online skill-building tutorials

Creative inspiration:

- DIY magazine subscriptions

- Access to project idea libraries

- Maker community memberships

Thoughtful homemade presents:

- Customized tool organizers

- Personalized toolbelts

- Framed photos of finished projects

Support meaningful causes:

- Affordable housing assistance

- Preserving historic buildings

- Teaching disadvantaged youth trades skills

Gifts for The Homebody

Cozy home accessories:

- Plush blankets and slippers

- Scented candles

- Custom throw pillows

Relaxation & entertainment:

- Audiobook subscriptions

- Board game packages

- Streaming service memberships

Creative activities:

- DIY craft supply boxes

- Macrame wall hanging kits

- Virtual cooking classes

Thoughtful homemade touches:
- Bath and body product baskets

- Knitted hats and scarves

- Photo collages

Support meaningful home causes:
- Sustainable building initiatives

- Organizations expanding food access

- Groups providing housing aid

Gifts for The Organizer

Handy tools:

Stylish pen holders

- Label makers

- Document scanners

Professional services:

- Decluttering specialists

- Productivity workshops

- Home organization apps

Inspirational resources:

- Audiobooks on organization

- Home organization podcasts

- Online organizing courses

Thoughtful DIY presents:

- Handmade cleaning caddies

- Personalized planners

- Custom storage bins

Support meaningful causes:

- Housing repair initiatives

- Workforce development programs

- Community sharing networks

Gifts for The Philanthropist

E ssentials for good:

- Fair trade gifts

- Ethical brand vouchers

- Charity news subscriptions

Insights & education:

- Social entrepreneurship workshops

- Documentary streaming services

- Books supporting good causes

Virtual generosity:

- Crowdfunding Donations

- Sponsor a child platforms

- Micro-giving gift cards

DIY infused with care:

- Charity greeting cards

- Upcycled accessory kits

- Homemade baked goods

Direct nonprofit support:

- Disaster relief organizations

- Hunger alleviation programs

- Environmental conservation funds

Gifts for The
Pragmatist

Useful essentials:

- Water bottles & hydration packs

- Noise-canceling headphones

- Premium kitchen tools

Handy services:

- Home organization specialists

- DIY & home improvement workshops

- Cloud file storage subscriptions

Educational resources:

- Audiobook memberships

- Online skill-building courses

- DIY magazine subscriptions

Thoughtful homemade gifts:
- Customized office organizers

- DIY self-care baskets

- Personalized cleaning kits

Worthy causes to support:
- Disaster relief funds

- Food banks & soup kitchens

- Workforce development programs

Gifts for The Sentimentalist

Cherished keepsakes:

- Custom jewelry with meanings

- Photo books capturing memories

- Personalized maps

Immersive experiences:

- Trips down memory lane

- Skill classes to share with the giftee

- Concert & event tickets

Virtual tributes:

- Online video messages

- Custom digital photo albums

- Nostalgic music streaming

Heartfelt DIY presents:

- Shadow boxes with mementos

- Handwritten letters

- Personalized memory jars

Donations honoring meanings:

- Disaster relief funds

- Animal welfare groups

- Veterans support organizations

Gifts for The Social Butterfly

Essentials for gatherings:

- Bluetooth speakers

- Outdoor movie screens

- Cocktail bar tools

Exciting experiences:

- Comedy show tickets

- Group fitness classes

- Food & wine tours

Creative connections:

- Language learning apps

- Video editing software

- Online gaming memberships

Thoughtful handmade touches:
- Custom friendship bracelets

- DIY photo booths

- Scrapbooks for memories

Support community bonds:
- Cultural exchange programs

- Social entrepreneurship funds

- Youth enrichment initiatives

Gift Ideas for Interests

Gifts that spark something special.

A Variety of Interests

G ifting based on interests allows honoring passions when personal details are lesser known. We explored present ideas for 10 popular pastimes to ignite inspiration:

Music lovers; Bookworms and literature aficionados; Fashionistas and style icons; Gamers and esports players; History buffs and genealogy enthusiasts; Stargazers and astronomy enthusiasts; Film and television aficionados; Writers, Photography enthusiasts; and Gardening and plant lovers.

Of course most people have many interests, but these categories create a foundation to relate. Some suggestions overlap, as certain gifts hold broad appeal across hobbyists.

With so many wondrous sides shaping our identities, consider these jumping off points rather than rigid definitions. Use intuition to gift in ways uplifting pastimes verbally expressed or silently cherished.

We hope these touchpoints allow giving even without familiarity to spread generosity through your community and beyond this season.

Gifts for Book Lovers

Reading essentials:
- Latest book releases

- eReaders

- Audiobook subscriptions

Bookish apparel & accessories:
- Literary-themed backpacks

- Booklover pins and bags

- Personalized bookmarks

Experiences for bibliophiles:
- Tickets to author events

- Bookstore or library tours

- Writing workshops

Online subscriptions:

- Book of the month clubs

- eBook rental services

- Book podcasts subscriptions

DIY and custom gifts:

- Handmade book sleeves

- Literary quote paintings

- Personalized book boxes

Charitable donations:

- Children's literacy programs

- Local library support

- Literary preservation funds

Gifts for Fashionistas

Stylish treats:

- Designer clothing & accessories
- Luxury handbags & shoes
- Subscription box with latest trends

Fashion insider access:

- Tickets to fashion shows
- Backstage passes & tours
- Personal styling sessions

Virtual gifts:

- Online personal shopping services
- Subscriptions to rental closets
- Virtual masterclasses & events

Sentimental DIY gifts:

- Custom jewelry & accessories

- Hand-painted denim jackets

- Upcycled statement pieces

Support ethical causes:

- Sustainable manufacturing initiatives

- Diversity & inclusion programs

- Educational opportunities for underserved designers

Gifts for Film Fanatics

Movie watching essentials:

Projectors and screens

- Surround sound systems

- Streaming subscriptions

Cinematic experiences:

- Film festival passes

- Movie studio tours

- Workshops with industry pros

Film lover memorabilia:

- Limited edition Blu-ray sets

- Vintage movie posters

- Themed clothing and accessories

Creative DIY gifts:

- Personalized movie scrapbooks

- Custom director fan art

- Handmade themed snack baskets

Support important cinema initiatives:

- Film preservation projects

- Diversity and inclusion programs

- Future filmmaker scholarships

Gifts for Gamers

Gaming gear & accessories:
- New consoles and VR headsets
- Handheld gaming emulators
- Custom controllers and keyboards

Gamer experiences:
- Tickets to gaming conventions
- Retro arcade trips
- Escape room adventures

Virtual gifts:
- Cloud gaming subscriptions
- Online coaching sessions
- Game design e-courses

Sentimental DIY gifts:

- Personalized controller skins

- Handmade electronic stands

- Custom gaming blankets

Support important causes:

- Digital literacy initiatives

- Preserving gaming history

- Promoting inclusion and accessibility

Gifts for Gardening Lovers

Essential gardening tools:

- Quality tool sets

- Gardening gloves

- Pruning shears

- Watering cans

Outdoor living accessories:

- Stylish sun hats

- Garden kneelers

- Decorative plant pots

Nurture their green thumb:

- Seed & seedling kits

- Gardening magazine subscriptions

- Online skill-building courses

Sentimental DIY gifts:
- Custom garden signs

- Handmade herb wreaths

- Personalized plant care packages

Support environmental causes:
- Community garden initiatives

- Pollinator conservation efforts

- Sustainable agriculture research

Gifts for History Lovers

Essential reads:

- Subscription to history magazines

- Local history books

- Collections of historical maps

Immersive experiences:

- Museum memberships

- Historical site tours

- Genealogy research trips

Virtual gifts:

- Ancestry website subscriptions

- History documentary streaming

- Online history lecture series

Thoughtful DIY gifts:

- Custom ancestral maps

- Family history scrapbooks

- Handmade heritage jewelry

Support important work:

- Historical preservation funds

- Archaeology research projects

- Cultural education initiatives

Gifts for Music Aficionados

For the concert and festival fan:

- Event tickets

- Backstage passes

- Music festival tickets

- Vinyl record subscription service

For the audiophile:

- Bluetooth speaker

- Headphones / earbuds

- Turntable

- Audio plugins or production tools

For the aspiring musician:

- Instrument lessons

- Sheet music journal

- Music composition software

- Virtual music lessons

Sentimental gifts:

- Photo album

- Custom guitar pick holder

- Framed song lyrics

Charitable donations:

- Music education programs

- Music therapy organizations

- Groups preserving musical heritage

- Festivals and venues in need

- Diversity and inclusion initiatives

Subscriptions and memberships:

- Streaming services

- Vinyl record clubs

- Online music publications

Gifts for Photography Lovers

Essential photography gear:

- New cameras and lenses

- Support accessories like tripods

- Photo printing services

Develop skills:

- Photography workshops

- Online tutorials and courses

- One-on-one mentoring sessions

Connect with the community:

- Tickets to gallery openings

- Photography conference passes

- Online photography groups

Thoughtful DIY gifts:

- Customized camera straps

- Handmade lens cleaning kits

- Personalized photo albums

Support important causes:

- Youth photography education

- Photojournalism projects

- Diversity and inclusion initiatives

Gifts for Stargazers

Essential gear:

- Telescopes for all skill levels

- Support accessories like tripods

- Filters to reduce light pollution

Cosmic experiences:

- Planetarium and observatory tickets

- Astronomy-themed travel tours

- Sky simulation apps

Celestial education:

- Books on astronomy topics

- Live virtual lectures

- Online courses to expand knowledge

Thoughtful DIY gifts:

- Handmade observation log journals

- Painted star charts

- Custom constellation quilts

Support the community:

- Fund astronomy education initiatives

- Preserve dark skies from light pollution

- Donate to spaces research and innovation

Gifts for Writers

Writing essentials:

Premium notebooks & journals

- Pens, pencils, and markers

- Portable writing bags

Develop the craft:
- Creative writing workshops

- How-to books and guides

- Editing software subscriptions

Connect with the community:
- Tickets to author readings

- Writing conference passes

- Online writing groups

Thoughtful DIY gifts:

- Personalized pen holders

- Handmade prompt idea jars

- Customizable notebooks

Support important literary causes:

- Youth writing education programs

- Underserved writers' funds

- Literary freedom & inclusion initiatives

Gift Lists for You

Thank you for your time

Thanks for giving!

The most meaningful gifts come from truly knowing someone's dreams. These printable pages help compile and organize presents for loved ones so thoughtfulness outshines stress.

You'll find:

- Shopping lists for jotting gift details and tracking spending

- A bonus wishlist template for recipients specifying their hopes if you wish to directly ask

After exploring suggestions elsewhere in the guide, use these pages to gather and compare concepts per person. Make notes on sizes, colors or variants that call to you. Tally proposed budgets so your generosity aligns with finances.

See this section as a practical toolkit honoring relationships through mindful curation rather than harried grabbing. My hope is simplifying empowers cherishing people, not just purchasing items.

Thank you for your dedication to meaningful giving! Wishing ease and inspiration carrying you through to joyful exchanges ahead. Now ready your gift list notepads and let the magical journey continue!

Gift List

NAME	GIFT	BUDGET	BOUGHT	WRAP

Gift
Questionnaire

Name: _______________________________

Favorite Things

COLOR: _______________________

PLACES TO SHOP: _______________________

COFFEE SHOP: _______________________

CANDY OR SNACKS: _______________________

RESTAURANTS: _______________________

HOBBIES OR ACTIVITES: _______________________

SCENTS: _______________________

DRINKS: _______________________

SPORTS TEAM: _______________________

MUSIC/ARTISTS: _______________________

FASHION ACCESSORIES: _______________________

TRAVEL DESTINATIONS: _______________________

AUTHORS/GENRES: _______________________

WILD CARD (ANYTHING!) _______________________

Practicalities

ALLERGIES OR SENSITIVITIES? _______________

____

CLOTHING AND SHOE SIZE: _______________

____

DON'T WANT/NEED: _______________

____

Preferences

	Y	N
COFFEE	☐	☐
TEA	☐	☐
MOVIE TICKETS	☐	☐
BOOKS	☐	☐
HOME DECOR	☐	☐
CANDLES	☐	☐
BATH PRODUCTS	☐	☐
SWEET	☐	☐
SAVORY	☐	☐
BAKED GOODS	☐	☐
INDOOR ACTIVITIES	☐	☐
OUTDOOR ACTIVITIES	☐	☐
ALCOHOL	☐	☐
CLOTHING	☐	☐
STATIONARY	☐	☐

Wish List

1. _______________________________

2. _______________________________

3. _______________________________